HOW TO PRAY SALAT

Quran Stories for Little Hearts

by

S A N I Y A S N A I N   K H A N

Goodword**kidz**

Helping you build a family of faith

One night a very strange and wonderful thing happened to the Prophet Muhammad ﷺ. This is known as *al-Isra* and *al-Miraj*, the Night Journey and the Ascension. The Angel Jibril (Gabriel) woke him up and took him on a strange white-winged animal, called Buraq (Lightning), from Makkah to the al-Aqsa Mosque in Jerusalem. From there he took the Prophet through the seven Heavens and finally into the divine Light of Allah's Presence. One of the commandments that Allah gave to the Prophet was to pray *(salat)* regularly. Allah wanted men to pray fifty times a day, but the Prophet begged Him to make it easing for everyone. At last Allah resolved that there should be five prayers a day. This shows the great importance of the five daily prayers.

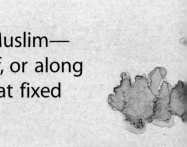

Therefore, *salat* is one of the five pillars of Islam. It is the duty of every Muslim—male and female—to perform the five daily prayers by himself or herself, or along with others in a congregation. All the five prayers have to be observed at fixed times. The names of the prayers and the times are as follows:

2

فجر

Fajr, or Early morning
prayer: two *rakahs,*
between dawn and
sunrise.

ظهر

Zuhr, or Noon prayer:
four *rakahs,* between
noon and mid-
afternoon.

عصر

Asr, or Afternoon prayer: four *rakahs,* between mid-afternoon and sunset.

مغرب

Maghrib, or Sunset prayer: three *rakahs,* between sunset and early evening.

عشاء

Isha, or Evening prayer: four *rakahs,* between the disappearance of twilight and the coming of the dawn.

"I have not created jinn and mankind for any other purpose except to worship Me."
The Holy Quran, 51:56

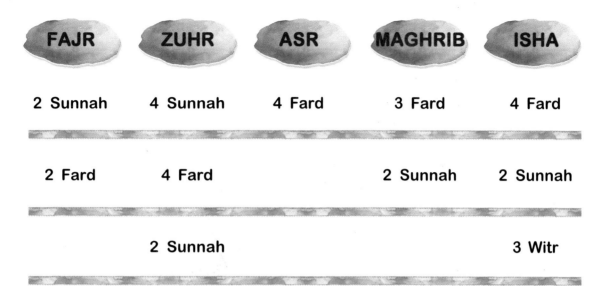

FAJR	ZUHR	ASR	MAGHRIB	ISHA
2 Sunnah	4 Sunnah	4 Fard	3 Fard	4 Fard
2 Fard	4 Fard		2 Sunnah	2 Sunnah
	2 Sunnah			3 Witr

The above table shows the *fard* (compulsory prayers) and *sunnah* (the Prophet's customary prayers). Everyone has to say these prayers. Apart from this, there are some more *sunnah* and *nafl* (voluntary) prayers which it is good to say as well.

"Recite what is sent of the Book to you, and perform regular Prayer: for Prayer restrains from shameful and evil deeds."
The Holy Quran, 29:45

ZUHR

NOON

ASR

SUNSET

SUNRISE

MAGHRIB

FAJR

MIDNIGHT

ISHA

Timings of Daily Prayers

To make yourself ready for *salat*, you would require to wash your face and arms, wipe your head and wash your feet.

Say: "Bismillah!" Wash both hands completely up to the wrist.

Rinse the mouth thoroughly.

Sniff water into the nose and blow it out.

Wash the face completely.

First wash your right hand and forearm, including the elbow.

Then wash your left hand and forearm, including the elbow.

This is called *wudu,* or ablution. There are twelve simple steps for doing *wudu*:

Pass both your wet hands over your head, from front to back and from back to front.

 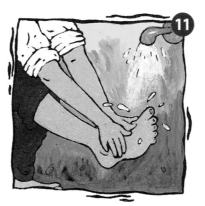 

Wipe your ears with your fingers from the inside out.

First wash your right foot thoroughly, including the ankle.

Then wash your left foot thoroughly, including the ankle.

After doing *wudu*, make known your intention to pray.

1 Raising your hands to your ears, say, "*Allahu akbar*" (اَللّٰهُ اَكْبَرُ) then place the right hand over the left hand on the navel.

2 Read "*Subhanaka Allahumma wa bi hamdika wa tabarakasmuka wa ta'ala jadduka wa la ilaha ghairuk.*

سُبْحَانَكَ اللّٰهُمَّ وَبِحَمْدِكَ وَتَبَارَكَ اسْمُكَ وَتَعَالٰى جَدُّكَ وَ لَآ اِلٰهَ غَيْرُكَ ۰

A'udhu billahi minash-shaitanir-rajim. Bismillahir-rahmanir-rahim."

اَعُوذُ بِاللّٰهِ مِنَ الشَّيْطٰنِ الرَّجِيْمِ ۰ بِسْمِ اللّٰهِ الرَّحْمٰنِ الرَّحِيْمِ ۰

Allah, all glory and praise belong to You alone. Blessed is Your name and exalted is Your Majesty, there is no god but You. I seek refuge in Allah from the cursed Satan. In the name of Allah, the Compassionate, the Merciful.

3 After this read, "*Alhamdu lillahi rabbil-alamin, ar-rahmanir-rahim. Maliki yawmiddin. Iyyaka na'budu wa iyyaka nasta'in. Ihdinassiratal-mustaqim. Siratal-ladhina an'amta 'alayhim, ghayril-maghdubi 'alayhim waladdallin. Amin.*"

اَلْحَمْدُ لِلّٰهِ رَبِّ الْعَالَمِيْنَ ۙ اَلرَّحْمٰنِ الرَّحِيْمِ ۙ مٰلِكِ يَوْمِ الدِّيْنِ ۰ اِيَّاكَ نَعْبُدُ وَاِيَّاكَ نَسْتَعِيْنُ ۰ اِهْدِنَا الصِّرَاطَ الْمُسْتَقِيْمَ ۙ صِرَاطَ الَّذِيْنَ اَنْعَمْتَ عَلَيْهِمْ ۙ غَيْرِ الْمَغْضُوْبِ عَلَيْهِمْ وَلَا الضَّآلِّيْنَ ۰ آمِين

1

2 **3**

Praise be to Allah, Lord of the Universe, the Compassionate, the Merciful, and Master of the Day of Judgement. You alone we worship, and to You alone we turn for help. Guide us to the straight path. The path of those whom You have favoured. Not of those who have incurred Your wrath, nor of those who have gone astray.

Now add one of the short surahs of the Quran, such as the surah al-Ikhlas:

"Qul huwallahu ahad. Allahussamad, lam yalid walam yulad, walam yakullahu kufuwan ahad."

قُلْ هُوَاللّٰهُ اَحَدٌ، اَللّٰهُ الصَّمَدُ،

لَمْ يَلِدْ وَلَمْ يُوْلَدْ، وَلَمْ يَكُنْ لَّهُ كُفُوًا اَحَدٌ،

Say: He is Allah, the One and Only, Allah, the Eternal, Absolute; He begot none, nor was He begotten. And there is none equal to Him.

4 Now say, *"Allahu akbar,"* (اَللّٰهُ اَكْبَرُ) bowing down and then say *Subhana rabbiyal 'azim* (سُبْحٰنَ رَبِّيَ الْعَظِيْمِ) three times.

5 Rising now to a standing position, say, *"Sami 'Allahu liman hamidah."* (سَمِعَ اللّٰهُ لِمَنْ حَمِدَهُ) or say, *"Rabbana lakal hamd,"* (رَبَّنَا لَكَ الْحَمْدُ) if you are praying behind an Imam.

14

4

5

6 Saying "*Allahu akbar*" (اَللّٰهُ اَكْبَرُ), prostrate yourself on the floor and say three times, "*Subhana rabbiyal 'ala*" (سُبْحَانَ رَبِّيَ الْاَعْلٰى).

7 Now rise to the seated position, saying, "*Allahu akbar*" (اَللّٰهُ اَكْبَرُ) and then again prostrate yourself and say three times, "*Subhana rabbiyal 'ala*" (سُبْحَانَ رَبِّيَ الْاَعْلٰى). Now get up, saying, "*Allahu akbar*" (اَللّٰهُ اَكْبَرُ). This completes one *rakah*. The second *rakah* will be performed in the same way, except that steps **1** and **2** will not be repeated.

After completion of the second *rakah*, sit upright and say:

8 "*At-tahiyyatu lillahi was-salawatu wat-tayyibat. As-salamu 'alaika ayyuhan-nabiyyu wa rahmatullahi wa barakatuh. Assalamu 'alayna wa 'ala 'ibadillahis-salihin. Ashhadu al la ilaha illallahu wa ashhadu anna Muhammadan 'abduhu wa rasuluh.*"

اَلتَّحِيَّاتُ لِلّٰهِ وَالصَّلَوَاتُ
وَالطَّيِّبَاتُ اَلسَّلَامُ عَلَيْكَ
اَيُّهَا النَّبِيُّ وَرَحْمَةُ اللّٰهِ وَبَرَكَاتُهُ
اَلسَّلَامُ عَلَيْنَا وَعَلَى عِبَادِ اللّٰهِ
الصَّلِحِيْنَ اَشْهَدُ اَنْ لَّاۤ اِلٰهَ اِلَّا اللّٰهُ
وَاَشْهَدُ اَنَّ مُحَمَّدًا عَبْدُهٗ وَرَسُوْلُهٗ

6

7

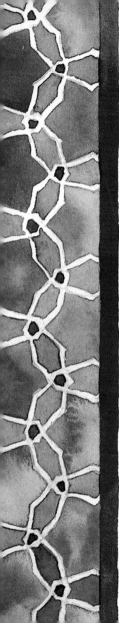

Salutation, prayers and good works are all for Allah. Let there be peace, Allah's mercy and blessings on you, O Prophet. Peace be on us and on all Allah's righteous servants. I testify that there is no god but Allah, and I testify that Muhammad is His servant and His Messenger.

If the prayer has more than two *rakahs*, stand up for the remaining *rakah*(s). If it is a two *rakah* prayer, remain seated and read:

"Allahumma salli 'ala Muhammadin wa 'ala ali Muhammadin kama sallayta 'ala Ibrahima wa 'ala ali Ibrahima innaka hamidum majid.

اَللّٰهُمَّ صَلِّ عَلَى مُحَمَّدٍ وَّعَلَى اللِ مُحَمَّدٍ كَمَا صَلَّيْتَ عَلَى اِبْرَاهِيْمَ وَعَلَى اللِ اِبْرَاهِيْمَ اِنَّكَ حَمِيْدٌ مَّجِيْدٌ

Allah, bless Muhammad and the family of Muhammad, as You blessed Ibrahim (Abraham) and his family, for You are the Praiseworthy and the Glorious.

Allahumma barik 'ala Muhammadin wa 'ala ali Muhammadin kama barakta 'ala Ibrahima wa 'ala ali Ibrahima innaka hamidum majid.

اَللّٰهُمَّ بَارِكْ عَلَى مُحَمَّدٍ وَّعَلَى اللِ مُحَمَّدٍ كَمَا بَارَكْتَ عَلَى اِبْرَاهِيْمَ وَعَلَى اللِ اِبْرَاهِيْمَ اِنَّكَ حَمِيْدٌ مَّجِيْدٌ

Allah, bless Muhammad and the family of Muhammad, as You blessed Ibrahim and the family of Ibrahim; for You are the Praised, the Magnified.

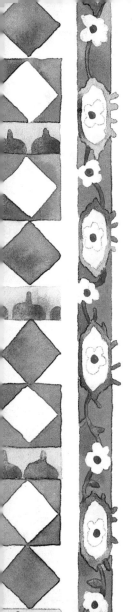

Allahumma inni zalamtu nafsi
zulman kathiran wa la yaghfirudh
dhunuba illa anta faghfirli
maghfiratam min 'indika warhamni
innaka antal ghafurur-rahim."

اَللّٰهُمَّ اِنِّي ظَلَمْتُ نَفْسِيْ ظُلْمًا
كَثِيْرًا وَّلَا يَغْفِرُ الذُّنُوبَ اِلَّا اَنْتَ
فَاغْفِرْلِيْ مَغْفِرَةً مِّنْ عِنْدِكَ وَارْحَمْنِيْ
اِنَّكَ اَنْتَ الْغَفُوْرُ الرَّحِيْمُ۰

Allah, I have been unjust to myself, too unjust. No one can grant pardon for my sins except You, so grant me Your forgiveness and have mercy on me, for You are the Forgiver, the Merciful.

9 **10** Now turn your face first to the right and then to the left, saying,

"Assalamu 'alaykum wa rahmatullah"

اَلسَّلَامُ عَلَيْكُمْ وَرَحْمَةُ اللهِ

This completes the prayer.

9

10

21

11 Now it is time for personal prayer. Here are some short prayers which are usually said at this time. You may pray on your own as well:

"Rabbana, atina fid-dunya hasanatan wa fil-akhirati hasanatan wa qina 'adhab an-nar."

رَبَّنَا آتِنَا فِى الدُّنْيَا حَسَنَةً وَّفِي الْآخِرَةِ حَسَنَةًوَّقِنَا عَذَابَ النَّارِ﮲

Our Lord, give us Good in this world and Good in the Hereafter, and save us from the torments of the fire.

"Rabbishrah li sadri wa yassir li amri."

رَبِّ اشْرَحْ لِيْ صَدْرِيْ وَيَسِّرْ لِيْ أَمْرِيْ﮲

O my Lord, expand my breast and ease my task for me.

"Rabbi zidni 'ilma".

رَبِّ زِدْنِيْ عِلْمًا﮲

O my Lord, increase my knowledge.

"Rabbighfir warham wa anta khayrur-rahimin."

رَبِّ اغْفِرْ وَارْحَمْ وَاَنْتَ خَيْرُ الرَّاحِمِيْنِ﮲

O my Lord, grant forgiveness and mercy, You are the best of those who are merciful.

11

Points to Remember

The aims of *salat* are:

1. to bring people closer to Allah;
2. to keep human beings from doing indecent, shameful and forbidden things;
3. to purify the heart, develop the mind and comfort the soul;
4. to remind people constantly of Allah and His greatness;
5. to develop discipline and will-power;
6. to guide people to the most upright way of life;
7. to show equality, unity and brotherhood;
8. to promote patience, courage, hope and confidence;
9. to train people in cleanliness, purity and punctuality;
10. to develop gratitude and humility;
11. to show obedience and thankfulness to our Creator.

Find Out More

To know more about the message and meaning of Allah's words, look up the following parts of the Quran which tell us about Salat:

Surah al-Baqarah 2:277, Surah an-Nisa 4:162, Surah al-Anfal 8:3, Surah ar-Ra'd 13:22-24
Surah al-Muminun 23:8-11, Surah an-Nur 24:56, Surah an-Naml 27:3,
Surah al-'Ankabut 29:45, Surah Luqman 31:4, Surah Fatir 35:29-30, Surah al-Ma'arij 70:34-35